Discard

Burmese and Malayan Cats

Burmese and Malayan Cats

Moira K. Swift

photographs by Animals Unlimited

BARRON'S

Woodbury, New York/London/Toronto/Sydney

Frontispiece A litter of kittens,
showing Browns, Blues, and
Platinums.

First U.S. Edition Published 1984
© Moira K. Swift 1983
British Edition published by
B. T. Batsford, Ltd.
4 Fitzhardinge St.
London W1H OAH

All inquiries should be addressed to:
Barron's Educational Series, Inc.
113 Crossways Park Drive
Woodbury, New York 11797

Author's Note
We should like to thank our many friends in the
Cat Fancy, without whom this book could not
have been written.

Acknowledgments are due to the Burmese Cat
Club for permission to reproduce material from
the Burmese Cat Club News and to the Cat
Fanciers' Association, Inc. for permission to
reproduce their Official Show Standards.

Library of Congress Catalog Card No. 84-14665
International Standard Book No. 0-8120-2925-9

Library of Congress Cataloging in Publication Data

Swift, Moira K.
  Burmese and Malayan cats.

  Includes index.
  1. Burmese cat.   I. Title.   II. Title: Malayan cats.
SF449.B8S95   1984   636.8'25   84-14665
ISBN 0-8120-2925-9

PRINTED IN ITALY

45   490   987654321

Contents

Introduction

It is difficult to believe that all the cat colors presented in this book descended from the brown-coated, yellow-eyed Burmese cat brought to the United States in 1930 by Dr. Joseph C. Thompson, a retired ship's doctor of the U.S. Navy. Obviously the cat was a novelty, being the only really brown one around! It soon became apparent that in time the beautiful glossy coat grew even richer in color, whereas the Siamese cat—the other Far-Eastern breed—was known to lose some of its gleaming appearance on becoming older.

The elegant and gentle Burmese cats, together with the closely related Malayans, are now popular the world over; in Britain they rank as the second largest group of pedigreed cats. In the United States, Burmese and Malayan cats are exceptionally popular too; no wonder, as it all started in the bungalow of Dr. Thompson in San Francisco, California.

From the outset you should visualize the cat you are going to read about—its size, shape, and color. Therefore the first section contains a summarized version of the "Standard" and a brief sketch of the behavior of the breeds.

Then we shall return to what is normally the beginning of any book on cats—the birth and foundation of the breed; its early history; the parting of the American cats from the British scene; the recognition of a separate breed, the Malayan, in the United States; and the ancestors of the English Burmese; their early owners, breeders, and judges. You will meet cats—some famous, some not at all well known but very important to the growth of the breed, including the early imports, from England to the United States, and their owners. This is a hitherto largely untold part of Burmese history—the story of the cats that followed the foundation stock and were the great- and the great-great-grandparents on the pedigrees of today's cats. Stories of them and their owners may bring nostalgia to elderly breeders and "show-goers."

Then follow the stories of the additional colors in which the original brown cats are now clothed, and the "link" cats to whom the imports were mated. These "link cats," some of which are still alive today, are not necessarily found in show catalogs or championship lists or recognized in any way publicly, but were, in the words of one breeder, "responsible for all the beautiful champion and grand champion cats to be found and recognized today." The history is enhanced with photographs.

Later in the book we will take a brief look at the world of cat shows, particularly from the point of view of the owner of the breeds; and introduce you to the joys and challenges of keeping a Burmese or Malayan cat in your home. There are some words of advice on whether to keep a stud. For detailed guidance on the breeding mother (queen) and kittening, you should consult one of the many detailed books already available. Care and grooming of Burmese and Malayan are much less laborious than that of longhairs, but a few words will be included on that subject too.

Many breeders and would-be breeders of Burmese and Malayans will wish to pursue the technical side of genetics and breeding; pertinent information is included in the appendices.

One

Appearance and Behavior

Burmese and Malayan cats have a striking appearance, with a rich gleaming coat. They are somewhat heavier in build than Siamese, and their muzzle is blunter. The American body type is slightly more muscular than the British.

Both breeds are shorthaired, long, elegant, of medium size, very hard and muscular, with a good weight for size (although it must be totally devoid of fat), a long neck, round chest, slender legs and neat oval paws. The tail is of medium length, straight, tapering slightly to a rounded tip. The particularly characteristic head is not of the long oriental type of the Siamese and associated breeds, which narrows on straight lines to a fine muzzle. The head of the Burmese and Malayan has the wedge, rounded on top, of medium length, that forms roughly an equilateral triangle to include the firm, strong chin, a definite nose break, and good breadth between the medium-to-large ears. The short coat is fine and silky and lies close to the body. Eye color is any shade of yellow from chartreuse to amber.

The following colors are registered in Britain: Brown (rich warm seal; slightly darker ears and face); Blue (soft silver-gray with distinct silver sheen); Chocolate (warm milk chocolate; ears and face slightly darker); Lilac (dove-gray with a slight pink overtone; ears and face darker); Red (light tangerine with slight tabby markings on face; ears distinctly darker) and Cream (rich cream). In all colors the underparts are lighter than the back.

There are also the so-called "new colors": Brown Tortie (a mixture of brown and red without any obvious barring); Blue Tortie/Blue Cream (a mixture of blue and cream without any obvious barring); Chocolate Tortie (a mixture of chocolate and red without any obvious barring) and Lilac Tortie/Lilac Cream (a mixture of lilac and cream, without any obvious barring). In the case of the four tortie colors, the coat may display two shades of each of its basic colors and may thus appear to have three or even four colors. The colors may be mingled or blotched; blazes, solid legs or tails are all permissible; therefore additional marks are awarded for type, which is of far greater importance than the coat color and markings.

In the United States Blue is called Malayan Blue, Chocolate is called Malayan Champagne and Lilac is called Malayan Platinum. The Malayan is regarded as a strictly American breed, officially recognized in 1980. In Great Britain the Malayan colors are considered Burmese. The Malayan breed has a fine, glossy, short, and satiny coat; the body is of medium size, muscular, compact, and devoid of fat. The chest is round and broad; the legs are slender. The breed has a pleasantly rounded head without flat areas, a very visible stop in profile and a full face.

Gr. Ch. Typha Dark Enigma, a Brown Burmese owned and bred by Rosemary Alger. Sire Ch. Braeside Woodhaze; dam Moorings Serena Sadie.

Gr. Pr. Kandi Niob Dinpar, a brown Burmese neuter male, illustrating the correct type as laid down by the Standard. Bred by Nigel Miller, by Ken Bayes' stud Samantoni Borzie Boy.

Matara Jambuua
showing the blue
coat of a Malayan.
Owned by Michael
Howard and bred by
Jay Moore. Sire Ch.
Anastra Spitfire; dam
Agpha Symmar.

Both breeds are usually very extroverted. Energetic, athletic, full of curiosity, brave, and adventurous, they are almost air-borne. The tops of furniture, high shelves and curtains are all quite usual places on which to rest, and to be achieved even when quite young. Knocking stored Christmas food from its safekeeping, turning on all the house lights, opening closed doors (no kind of handle an obstacle), turning knobs by swinging on them, having to be rescued by the fire department from the tops of trees, answering the telephone by knocking the receiver off the hook—the list can be extended to include many very funny and some quite astonishing items that are an indication of living habits.

Burmese and Malayans become very attached to owners, walking with them, sleeping on them, sharing their beds, rather dangerously traveling with them in cars (sometimes to be lost when emerging in some strange district). They mix well with other animals after a fairly long preliminary trial period. As to their own offspring, usually Burmese and Malayan queens are the most attentive of mothers, refusing to leave the babies at all, but adamant as to where they are going to keep them—not in the least where you expect or want.

Burmese are full of curiosity. This Malayan Champagne kitten is chasing a bee.

Although capable of climbing to great heights, this Malayan Platinum kitten is having difficulty getting down from the tree top.

Two
The Early History of the Burmese/Malayan Cats

Although shrouded by lack of information, the beginning of the Burmese breed has been sketched in many books on cats and has been accompanied by such carefully retouched photos as did exist. The notes and the photos cannot vary, since there is only one factual story.

The early development of the breed took place largely on the West Coast of the U.S., in the hands of Dr. Joseph C. Thompson, who in 1930, took from Burma to San Francisco a small brown female which he called Wong Mau (always described as "a little brown cat"). Apart from Dr. Thompson there are other names that appear in the earliest records: Mrs. Billie Gerst (Gerstdale), Mrs. Mildred Alexander (Mrs. Alexander), Miss Winifred Porter (The Farm), Mr. Guy Fisher (Forbidden City), Mr. and Mrs. Howard Warren (Casa Gatos), among others. Also on the East Coast cattery names appeared: Newton (Mrs. Virginia Cobb), Chindwin (Mr. and Mrs. E. Battey), Laos and Yana (Mrs. Donald Came), Tang Wong (Mrs. M.G. Stevens), Cummings (Mrs. E.L. Cummins), and Miss Burns (Mrs. Lilian W. Burns).

Mrs. Gerst (Gerstdale) became well known for her virile and healthy cats, produced mainly by inbreeding, as she apparently did not buy stock from other breeders. Mrs. Stevens in Seattle owned—for a while—the famous Wong Mau as well as her daughter Wong Mau II, and Mrs. Stevens also became known for her fine stock.

One cat, named Chango, of the cattery of Miss Porter, became famous in Britain. He was a hybrid, born in 1941. His father was a Siamese cat, his mother a pure Burmese. Prior to his departure to England he mated two Siamese, while shown in Boston. Those two Siamese females were Mrs. Battey's Chindwin's Minkee, and Mrs. Came's Yana's Minga. There was one Siamese in each litter, and one male and two female hybrids. Mrs. Came and Mrs. Battey exchanged the male hybrids in order to develop a new line. When Mrs. Came gave up her cattery in 1950, the majority of her cats were taken by Mr. and Mrs. Howard Warren, Idyllwild, California. For many years Mr. Warren was president and Mrs. Warren secretary of the Burmese Cat Society.

Ch. Qualitas Jiminy
Cricket, a Malayan
Platinum owned and
bred by David and
Heather Neil; bred
from Bambino Beau
Geste, he was their
first Champion.

A Malayan Platinum
Champion: Ch.
Phthazzar Lilac Laird,
owned by Ann and
Alan Fullwood and
bred by Mr. and Mrs.
Frazer. Sire Ch. Vatan
Cream Adonis; dam
Deucalion Orthia.

17

Ch. Patriarca Praline Pintado, a Malayan Champagne owned and bred by Pat Brownsell. Sire Kanzan Chocolate Chico; dam Patriarca Prunella.

In our book *The Burmese Cat* (Silkstone Richard, Pocock, Swift and Watson, Charles Scribner, New York, 1979) we state: "In 1942, three more cats reached America from Rangoon, imported on behalf of Mr. Guy Fisher, but only one of these, Tangyi, seems to appear in early Burmese pedigrees.

The breed was first recognized by the American Cat Fanciers' Association (CFA) in 1936. By 1946 some Burmese were achieving major success at shows, but in

1947 the breed received a severe setback when the CFA suspended its recognition of the Burmese. It is difficult now to appreciate the full effect of this on Burmese breeders of the day, and it is possible only to speculate why it happened. It must be appreciated that, at the time, the cats available to American breeders were only a few generations removed from the original imports and the necessary crosses of them with Siamese; as a result, the number of pure breeding cats was very small. It appears that Tangyi of Forbidden City, one of the 1942 imports, was regarded by breeders as being pure Burmese because she was dark in color, although . . . it seems far more likely that she would in fact have been an abnormally dark-coated hybrid." Also, from articles which appeared at the time, it seems that some breeders had genuine difficulty in distinguishing between pure Burmese and Burmese/Siamese hybrids and that others deliberately exploited the situation by producing hybrids and passing them off as pure Burmese. This led to the Burmese Cat Society of America requiring prospective members to show that they understood the difference between a pure Burmese and a Burmese/Siamese hybrid and to give an assurance that they would sell as Burmese only true Burmese cats. As often happens, this setback proved to be beneficial, for the severe jolt administered by the loss of breed recognition caused more responsible breeders to intensify their efforts to extend the breed and improve the cats they were producing. It was during this period that Sin Gu of Forbidden City and So Wat of Forbidden City were born, both of whom appear in the pedigrees of the British Foundation cats. By 1953 the situation had improved sufficiently for the CFA to restore recognition (the other three registration bodies—Cat Fanciers' Federation (CFF), United Cat Fanciers (UCF), and American Cat Association (ACA)—had not withdrawn their recognition in 1947).

Prior to 1958 the interests of American Burmese breeders had been looked after by the Burmese Cat Society (BCS) in the East, and the Burmese Breeders of America (BBA), consisting of breeders in the West. In 1958 both societies merged: the United Burmese Cat Fanciers (UBF). In 1954, CFA accepted the Burmese standard of points for Brown (produced in 1951 by the BCS). However, many American associations, including the CFA, recognize as Burmese only the Browns or Sables. In other associations recognition is given to Champagne (Chocolate), Platinum (Lilac) and, more recently and somewhat reluctantly, Blues. In the CFA, cats of these colors with Burmese ancestry are to be registered, known, and shown as "Malayan"; Red, Cream, and Tortie are not recognized at all as Burmese, since they are regarded as hybrids.

It is known that ever since the establishment of the Burmese breed in the United States, colors other than brown appeared in a few brown litters. The existence of champagne colors was acknowledged, even though the cats were discarded as hybrid. Those that appeared "blue" disappeared or were not mentioned at all. It is now known that as early as 1947, a blue kitten called So Wat appeared in a litter, along with a brown. In 1953 a litter that included Casa Gatos Darkee also included a blue kitten. Casa Gatos Darkee was sold to England and there mated back to one of his daughters, Ch. Chinki Golden Gay, producing the first blue kitten, Sealcoat Blue Surprise.

In the U.S., under CFA rules, the registration of litters is still at the option of

Two cats important in the history of the breed: left, Ch. Laos Cheli Wat (female); right, Casa Gatos da Foong (male). (*Associated Newspapers*)

the breeder. Litters may be registered either as Malayan or as Burmese, both parents in either case being registered Burmese. There are four color varieties for both Malayan and Burmese, and one special category for Burmese, only for show purposes. Only Blue, Champagne, and Platinum may be shown as Malayan. Sable (Brown) may *not* be shown as Malayan. To be shown it must be registered as Burmese and comes in the separate category for show purposes. It had been proposed that any brown kitten in a Malayan litter would be known as AOV Chocolate Malayan, but this is not yet re-

solved. In a Burmese litter, any kittens other than brown will be transferred and reregistered, and the Sable (Brown) kittens will remain Burmese. Burmese cats with red, cream, or tortie in their background are not eligible to be registered for either breed, since only naturally occurring colors are permitted.

To sum up, a cat of certain colors may be known as Burmese in Britain and as Malayan under the rules of some of the American registering bodies. In general, Australia, New Zealand, and Europe follow the British practice.

Three
The Development of the Breed

In the previous chapter we said that the first Burmese was imported from Burma to the U.S. by Dr. J.C. Thompson. According to travelers' reports brown cats were quite rare.

It is assumed that Burmese are a very old breed indeed, and were kept only by the wealthy, or in the temple. In the latter case they were regarded as sacred animals. There they were cared for by specially trained servants who could be severely punished if harm came to those cats. Because of this special care, the purity of the breed could also be maintained. The only possible way to obtain a brown cat in those days was if such an animal was presented as a gift to important people.

The story goes that Dr. Thompson was at one time a Buddhist monk in a Lama monastery in Tibet. It was, however, much later that he acquired the now famous Wong Mau; at that time he was a practicing psychiatrist in San Francisco, breeding cats in his spare time. Although many American breeders regarded Wong Mau as a very dark Siamese, of Malay type, Thompson was of a completely different opinion, and together with three breeders who were well educated in genetics, Thompson started a series of experimental breeding projects, in order to reveal the genetic makeup of Wong Mau. In the Appendix on page 58 you will find the classic paper by Thompson and his associates, published in the American *Journal of Heredity* in 1943. They proved that Wong Mau was a Siamese hybrid with a coat of new color: brown. They called the breed "Burmese" because of Wong Mau's origin. As a result of their research it also became possible to segregate this brown-coated variety, and as such, the breed was recognized by the Cat Fanciers' Association of America in 1936. The first brown cats were called "Sable Burmese" in the U.S. and "Brown Burmese" in Britain.

The Burmese carries a color restriction gene, like the Siamese; however, the Burmese gene is less effective. Burmese kittens show defined points that tend to disappear or reduce in intensity as the young cats become older. Only in extremely dark brown Burmese can these points remain in evidence.

The first three all brown Burmese cats were imported by Sydney and Lillian France from the U.S. to Britain in 1949. They were:

Chindwins Minou Twm (f) ♀

Ch. (U.S.A.) Laos Cheli Wat (f) ♀

Casa Gatos da Foong (m) ♂

These three cats were obtained from Mrs. Blanche Warren of Idyllwild, California,

one of the most important early American breeders of Burmese. The three cats were genetically unrelated and of the best breeding stock then available. One of the cats, Cheli, had won her American championship under the CFF in 1948, was the best colored and best Burmese in the CFF Brooklyn Long Island Cat Club Show in 1947, and came in third in the ACA Southern California SH Breeders Show in 1948. According to *The Burmese Cat,* Cheli subsequently proved not to be in kitten, but Minou was, and her kittens were born in quarantine at Tamworth in Staffordshire, England.

These three cats were followed in 1953 by Casa Gatos Darkee (m).

In 1954 Mrs. France transferred all her Burmese to Mrs. C. F. Watson, who three years later imported from the U.S. the brown Darshan Khudiram (m).

No significant crossbreeding took place. Vic Watson, founder of the Burmese Cat Club, considers that; if carried out in a carefully controlled way, it would have been a legitimate way of creating badly

Opposite

Gr. Ch. Kayserling Kerena and her daughter Ch. Kayserling Katie Blue. Both these cats, bred by Anne Budge, stem from the Canadian stud Gr. Ch. Halton Ridge Alfie.

Two beautiful Malayan Blues bred by Miss Moira Mack: Belcanto Daphne, and Belcanto Little Leela.

needed new bloodlines, but the breeders of the day, who were small in number and intensely loyal to the breed, were totally opposed to extending the breeding lines in this way. Some of the very earliest of prefixes are still to be found in the "back lines" of a great number of today's cats. The last of Khudiram's daughters, Kutkai Shila, died only in 1982 at the age of 18¼.

The cats of these breeders were the foundation stock of the breed until the arrival of the Canadians in 1968 (with the exception of Mrs. Grove-White's Chira Tan Tockseng in 1958). Some famous prefixes of the time are: Chinki, Sablesilk, Kyneston, Lamont, Sealcoat, Kathoodu, Fernreig, Kingsplay, Nilgiris, Kachin, Dewpoint, Silverseal. The import from Canada was significant because it brought with it some changes in appearance and type that some people considered very much to the benefit of the breed. Certainly, improved eye color and warmth of coat can be so attributed. In 1968, Dr. E. Allen took to Canada her brown queen Dormin Psyche, where she was mated to two Canadian studs. Ch. Wai-Ling Phantom of Fredra's and Gr. Ch. Halton Ridge Alfie of Silkwood. A brown female, Tapawingo Beothuk, was born in Canada, and mated to her son before coming home to England where kittens were born in quarantine. One of these, Tapawingo Shoshone, became a stud. Here began the long and wide use of Tapawingos as studs and queens, and the prefix became very well known. The Canadian cats, as well as showing good eye color, had brighter, warmer coats than their English fellows, and this has become part of a desirable standard.

It was Casa Gatos Darkee who, when mated back to one of his daughters, Ch. Chinki Golden Gay, produced the first blue kitten, Sealcoat Blue Surprise. Blue Surprise herself never produced a blue kitten.

Without deeply discussing genetics (dealt with more fully in an appendix), it may be interesting to learn how we actually see the colors of cats. The colors we see depend on the light bounced back from the surface of color granules on each hair. These granules, through a complicated chemical process, occur in each hair as it comes through the skin, and we see different colors because the light reflected is affected by the location, shape (e.g., round in black cats), and quantity of the granules.

From the 1950's onwards we now know that blue cats or cats that looked "blue" did appear in sable litters in the United States and in Britain. So far for the most part, blissfully unaware of the long battle that was to be waged on the other side of the Atlantic as to the possible existence of "blue Burmese," the small English Burmese fraternity watched and counted with happiness and pride the kittens with a different-colored body, and a quite unmistakable blue fringe to their ears. Stud owners, often after violent disbelief and sometimes acrimonious conversations with excited owners of queens, ventured to amend their advertisements to "brown Burmese, carrying blue." The breed number 27a was allocated upon GCCF recognition of the Blue Burmese in 1960, and the Standard of Points was amended. Many people agreed that they were very pretty kittens, but there was considerable discussion also about the shade of blue and its description in the Standard of Points. It was eventually agreed in the form: "In maturity the adult should be a soft silvery grey only slightly darker on the back and tail. There should be a distinct silver sheen

on rounded areas such as ears, face and feet. Nose leather very dark grey, foot pads grey."

Producing blues seemed to demand a pedigree traceable through HRH Marin Szam-Gru and HRH Marin Sirocco to Sable Shadow Milord of HRH Marin, a generation earlier in the extended pedigrees of two of the American groups sold to Britain. The latter certainly appears among the forebears of both Aybo Budda and Belfort Belcanto Le Coq d'Or, brought in by Elizabeth Caldicott and Moira Mack respectively.

It is worth noting that nearly as many differences existed in the color of the Blues as in the color of Chocolates later, but the Blues were very clearly divided into the sources from which they could be traced, e.g., first the darker, pewter color of those Americans closely connected with Darkee; then the different blues from the Canadian infusion; and finally the much lighter, more silvery but much more lilacy blue springing from the Malayan Champagne and Malayan Platinum studs such as Ch. Milbuyo Le Marquis, and others from the last American imports.

We owe much of the present beauty and elegance to the cats that link the early breeding stock to the later developments involving the new colors described in the next section. Many of these cats did not appear frequently on the show bench, as most of their hard work was in the breeding pens as studs or queens, but they should not be forgotten.

It is interesting to note how studs have been chosen and used over the years. At first breeders confined themselves largely to the foundation stock and its immediate offspring. Naturally, too, they were anxious to use new studs—even though cautious until something of the resulting kittens and colors was known. The result was that whereas in the past the same names would appear and reappear in the catalogs, as parents of the kittens on show, from about 1970 a large selection of new names and owners appeared. At the same time some well-known stock disappeared from the show scene; and indeed often the new studs disappeared from prominence quickly, having being used only once or twice. Among the newcomers in Britain were some of the very beautiful Creams and Reds which had been bred in seclusion—their story comes next in Chapter Four—and one or two of the early Malayan Champagne and Malayan Platinum imports to Britain from the U.S.

As time went on this unfamiliar collection of strangers from the U.S. sorted itself out into those, whatever their color, with the Burmese type, and those without. The descendants of the early entrants in the stud book are still with us today. In only a few years there were some Champions and/or Grand Champions in some of the colors; by 1981 the only two colors without a Grand Champion were Chocolate and Lilac-Tortie. The type of nearly all the Tortie Champions is magnificent. In the U.S., however, in 1980, the Chocolate (Champagne) and Lilac (Platinum) were officially recognized and regarded as a strictly American breed: the Malayan.

Four

Red, Cream, Tortoiseshell, Champagne, and Platinum

It is well known that in some American associations the only color recognized as Burmese is the Sable, or Brown. The colors Red, Cream, and Tortie are not recognized at all as Burmese, since they are regarded as hybrids. Be this as it may, there is nevertheless a lot of truth in what the English cat breeder and founder of the Burmese Cat Club, Mr. Vic Watson, says when he states that it is one of the facts of genetics, that inheritance of color (and the blue dilution factor that modifies a color) is not directly linked to coat pattern and type. It is therefore possible to substitute one color for another without the basic characteristics and type being changed. A cat in which the normal brown has been diluted to blue, or the genetic black color substituted by red or chocolate (champagne), is just as much a Burmese as its brown counterpart. In fact, this line of reasoning is parallel to that followed in the Siamese cat world, where the original imported cats were sealpointed (corresponding genetically to the Brown Burmese), but bluepoints, chocolatepoints, lilacpoints and so on have been developed as the result of color substitution and dilution. It is accepted in both Britain and the United States that these color variants are just as fully Siamese cats as the original sealpoints. It is therefore difficult to understand why Burmese cats are treated differently from Siamese.

It is more than appropriate in this book to discuss three extremely important colors, known for their beauty and popularity. Red and Cream were created—between 1965 and 1975—by Mrs. Robine Pocock and Mrs. Joyce Dell. These sex-linked colors evolved from the use of a Red Tabby and a Siamese to introduce the color, and culminated by careful selective breeding, with cats of beautiful pure clear coats and excellent type that appeared on the show bench a few years before the appearance of the Champagne (and/or Platinum) color.

Cream is a dilution of red. The cat has a light, clear coat in Reds and Creams, and the nose leather and foot pads of both

Ch. and Pr. Braeside
Red Admiral, owned
and bred by Helen
Hewitt. Sire Ch.
Cavcots Creighton;
dam Fleetfoot Sophy.
The black spots on
the cat's nose would
disqualify him at an
American show.

Kupro Cream
Tinkerbelle, a cream
female owned and
bred by Joyce Dell.
Sire Gr. Ch. Rascals
Butterscotch; dam
Kupro Cream
Coquette.

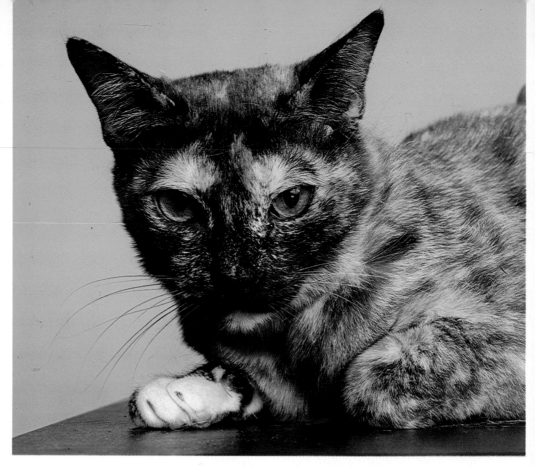

Ch. and Gr. Pr. Pussinboots Razzamatazz, a Brown British Tortie owned and bred by Robine Pocock, who has made great contributions to the breeding of the sex-linked colors. Sire Ch. Braeside Golden Promise; dam Kevitor Brown Kelowna.

Previous page, left
A Blue British Tortie: Bergil Burata, owned and bred by Don Beech and Jim Chalmers. Sire Gr. Ch. Kupro Cream Rama; dam Grandoak Jasmine.

Previous page, right
The first lilac (-platinum) British Grand Champion, Gr. Ch. Cavaquinto, owned by Jeff Lenehan and bred by Dawn Hadley. The list of his show successes includes six Best in Show wins. Sire Ch. Mibuya Le Marquis; dam Elidor Cobweb.

are pink. Sometimes people are confused by the two varieties. The ears of a Red are distinctly darker than the back of the cats, whereas the ears of the Cream are only a very little darker than the back and have a "dusted" look. In the early days two distinctly different looking lines of both Red and Cream were produced: on the one hand came svelte cats with longer legs and bodies, and on the other stockier cats with shorter thicker tails, but over a period of ten years' breeding these were integrated and the elegant Reds and Creams of today were produced.

Also very attractive are the Torties. When Red or Cream males mate with any Brown, Blue, Chocolate (Champagne) or Lilac (Platinum) females, then a percentage of the resulting litters will contain some Tortoiseshell females. No two Torties are alike. Their coloring may be patched or intermingled, and individual coloring is interesting and very attractive. The solid colors are brown/red, chocolate/red, blue and cream, and lilac and cream, but the red may be so light a red as to appear cream or almost white. It is, however, quite definitely light red.

Sabra Honeybun is typical of the Chocolates (Champagnes) bred from the early American imports.

The type of Torties is a most important factor, since they are one of the important links in the relationship between the sex-linked group and the basic colors of the brown/blue group. Examine the pictures with this in mind; there are some beautiful examples of heads. The genetics of the Tortoiseshell factor are discussed in a short note in an appendix at the end of the book, on page 58.

The appearance of two distinct shades of color in both Champagne (Chocolate) and Platinum (Lilac), but primarily in Champagne, caused great controversy. Color resulting from mating Champagne with Champagne (Chocolate with Chocolate) differed from matings where a Brown sire was used. Where Blue was involved, there were even further very marked differences in the depth of resulting Champagne. Mating Platinum to Platinum (Lilac to Lilac) sometimes produced a very light Lilac, almost Cream. A very wide range of Champagne (Chocolate) must be accepted. The reduction of the difference in depth of color between face (mask) and body is being achieved. In short: the Malayan Platinum represents

33

Cilla Snowpaws, a
British Lilac Tortie
owned by Toni Smith
and bred by Ruth
Helliwell. Sire Typha
Ahmed Beauty; dam
Hildegard
Hildewilde.

the blue dilution of champagne (chocolate) and is the result of mating two cats both carrying champagne (chocolate) *and* blue genes. And as far as the Malayan Champagne is concerned, it is more than likely that "either the genetic brown or chocolate was deliberately introduced (through crossing CP Siamese, and interbreeding the hybrids), or that the genetic brown or chocolate (champagne) came in with the original Burmese/Siamese hybrids or Siamese used in the original breeding program and, as with the blue dilution of brown, apparently remained unexpressed for some time. There is evidence to support this theory. An American champagne (chocolate UK) pedigree of more than ten years ago shows the genetic brown gene on one side and it must have been present on the other to operate the pedigree." (See *The Burmese Cat*).

Malayan Platinum is a delicate dove-gray pale color with a slightly pinkish cast (faded effect). The platinum (lilac) color changes with age. Champagne kittens and Platinum kittens are, at birth, indistinguishable, but when approximately three weeks old, white appears in the platinum and cream in the champagne.

Five
The Show Scene

When planning to take part in a show, usually a two-day affair, be wise and pick a show that is within easy driving distance of your home. The first step is writing to the secretary of the club who organizes the show, asking for an entry form. The entry blank then must be filled out properly; in case of a show affiliated with, for instance, the CFA, not only the name of the organizing club must be given on the form, but also in which class the cat is to be entered: Nonchampionship, Championship, or Premiership. Those three classes are in turn divided into subclasses. The show rules of the CFA define the following:

Nonchampionship Classes

a) The *Kitten Class* is for any kitten, male or female, not less than 4 months old but under 8 calendar months old on the opening day of the show, which, if an adult, would be eligible to compete in a Championship Class. Kittens are not eligible for any "Best" in show except Kitten awards.

b) The *AOV* (Any Other Variety) *Class* is for any registered, adult, whole cat or registered kitten, the ancestry of which entitles it to Championship competition, but which does not (because of color, coat, or, in case of Manx, because of its tail) conform to the accepted show standard. An AOV entry is eligible for awards only in the AOV class of its own breed.

c) The *Provisional Breed Class* is for any registered cat or registered kitten of a breed not accepted for Championship competition, when CFA has approved a provisional standard for that breed. Cats entered in the PBC are eligible for awards only in the PBC. Provisional Breeds shall compete separately as Kittens, Altered Cats, or Adult, whole cats.

d) The *Miscellaneous* (Noncompetitive) *Class* is for any registered cat or registered kitten of a breed not yet accepted for Provisional Breed competition.

e) The *Household Pet Class* is for any domestic kitten or altered cat entry not otherwise eligible. Household pets are eligible only in the Household Pet Class. Household pets are to be judged separately from all other cats, solely on beauty and condition. Feral cats or feral cat-domestic cat hybrid crosses are not eligible for entry.

Championship Classes

a) The *Open Class* is for CFA registered cats of either sex, 8 months or over, except cats that have completed requirements for Championship confirmation. When a cat has completed requirements for confirmation, it is ineligible for the Open Class at any subsequent show.

b) The *Champion Class* is for cats that have completed Championships in this Association, and for which the required Championship claim has been mailed to the Central Office.

c) The *Grand Champion Class* is for cats that have completed Grand Championship in CFA.

Premiership Classes

a) Premiership Classes are for CFA registered neutered or spayed cats, 8 months old or over, that would, as whole cats, be eligible to compete in the Championship classes.

b) The following classes will be recognized for neuters and spays of each Champhionship Color Class: Grand Premier, Premier, and Open. The eligibility of each class will be determined in the same manner as for the corresponding class in Championship competition.

Wins made in Championship competition may not be transferred to Premiership records. However, titles won in Championship competition are retained.

When is a cat eligible for entry? According to CFA: "Any cat or kitten of sound health not less than 4 calendar months old on the opening day of a show sanctioned by CFA." Any cat or kitten, however, from a house or cattery where there has been fungus or any infectious or contagious illness within twenty-one days prior to the opening date of a show is, of course, ineligible for entry, and should entry have been made prior to the onset of any such condition, such entry is ineligible for admission into the showroom. It is understood that only cats registered with CFA are eligible for entry in the different classes.

It is the responsibility of the owner to enter the cat with its proper registration number as shown on the registration certificate.

When an officiating judge is the breeder of a cat or kitten, such cat or kitten is not eligible for competition in that judge's ring. This rule does not apply to shows in Hawaii and Japan.

A neutered or spayed kitten is not eligible for entry.

A cat that has completed requirements for Championship or Premiership confirmation is ineligible for further competition until claim has been filed for Championship or Premiership.

A cat that has won a Championship or Premiership in one color class is not eligible for entry in a different color class except that a cat that has been confirmed as a Champion or Premier in one color class and, after confirmation, changes color, may be shown in the correct color class by notifying the Central Office of the color change and payment of a fee. The cat may then compete as an open in the proper class. The central Office must confirm the color class change prior to competition in a new color class. Only one change will be permitted.

A cat not having all its physical properties—eyes, ears, legs, tail, claws, for example—is not eligible for entry, subject to the following exceptions: a) cats in Premiership classes have been altered; and b) altered cats are eligible for adult Household Pet classes.

An adult male must have at least one descended testicle to be eligible for entry. Male kittens, however, are not required to have descended testicles.

The Show Committee may refuse to accept any entry received after midnight of the advertised date for the closing of entries, or after the advertised limit of number of entries has been reached.

The Show Committee may permit kittens 4 months old or older, or cats, to be shown for sale.

No more than two kittens or one cat may be benched in a single cage, whether entered for exhibition, for sale, or for competition.

No cat or kitten shall be benched at more than one show per week (Monday through Sunday inclusive).

Judging at one of today's English shows.

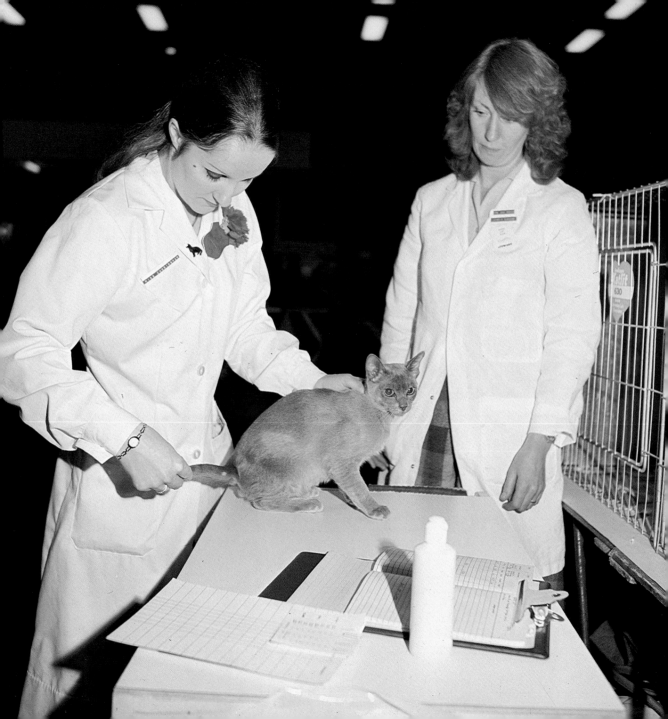

The first British Premier Chocolate Burmese, Pr. Typha Ahmini Bambi. Bred by Rosemary Alger. Sire Kernow Kedron; dam Moorings Serena Sadie.

Opposite left
Gr. Ch. Vintage Wyvem was in the first litter bred in England by Pat Gummow; he was a Champion at 10½ months, a Grand Champion at 15 months and 10 days—one of the youngest Burmese Grand Champions.

Opposite, right
Pr. Maichiang Mishmis, an English blue neutered female owned by Rosemary Hall and bred by Michael Howard. Some of the loveliest Burmese can be found in the neuter sections of shows. Strong family resemblance can be seen with her parents, Ch. Jingpaws Blue Monarch and Matara Jambuua, both illustrated in this book.

Opposite, below
Mrs. Frances Williams' "Moorings" prefix can be found in the pedigrees of many famous cats today: this is Moorings Serena Sadie, the foundation queen of Rosemary Alger's "Typha" cats. Sire Suda Sirocco Simon; dam Ramree Ahminah.

From the foregoing it is apparent that it is important to fill in the entry blank properly before returning it to the secretary of the organizing club. And don't forget to pay the entry fee! An entry must be the property of the person who is shown on the entry blank as the owner. The records in the Central Office are conclusive where the ownership of the entry is concerned. If title is transferred between the date of entry and the date of the show, the transfer must be reported to the Show Secretary. It is essential that transfer of ownership papers be filed with the Central Office immediately upon transfer of title. It is also necessary to clip the claws of each entry prior to benching.

Depending upon the rules of the organizing cat association or federation— and most show rules are simple and straightforward—the health of your cat has to be certified by a veterinarian on arrival at the show. It is advisable to know exactly what is expected, so be well informed! The CFA is quite clear about health requirements. It advises strongly that before entry a licensed veterinarian inoculate your cat or kitten against feline enteritis, feline rhinotracheitis, and calici viruses.

The CFA, founded in 1906, is by far the largest registering body in the U.S., having more than 575 member clubs, and being responsible for more than half the vast number of shows in the U.S. The great geographical distances in the United States made it impracticable to have only one body registering and sponsoring shows, and other organizations evolved. Several of the federations have banded together and are collectively known as the International Cat Associations. At their shows they accept cats registered with any association, which helps the exhibitors considerably; otherwise cats must be registered with the specific organization running the show they wish to enter.

Fortunately the standards are very much the same throughout the U.S., as is the system of running the show, which differs considerably from that in Britain. The most prestigious shows in the United States are usually held between September and February.

A cat has to be familiarized with its show-type cage. Even more important of course is to bring the animal into top condition. Check its ears, clip its claws, and clean its body so it is free from dirt and fleas. It is understood that an obviously pregnant female cat doesn't belong at a show.

In general it is advisable to isolate cats for at least two weeks prior to the show, in order to prevent possible contagious diseases.

A couple of hours before the show the cat should not receive any food, but as soon as it is placed in its show cage, and the animal has settled down, some of its favorite light food (snack) can be presented.

When you arrive in the show hall, one of the officials will hand you a card on which your name, your cat's name, and the number of its cage are typed. You will also get a schedule of the various classes, and the names of the, usually four, judges and their location in the show hall.

As soon as your cat is examined and certified by a veterinarian (if a vet is assigned to the show) and safely placed in its show cage, it is wise to purchase a catalog, so you will know who your competitors are.

After your cat is comfortable, it is time to locate the place where your cat will be judged. This "ring" is a large table with a small platform, behind which the judge

sits. On either side, behind the judge, is a U-shaped line of about 10 cages in which the cats will be placed by a steward prior to judging. At one side of that same table sits a clerk who keeps records, enters your name, and checks all the information against the notes in the catalog.

The judge has a looseleaf notebook in which all entries are properly recorded. Then each class is called on the loudspeaker, and the cats placed in the cages behind the judge. Attached to the front of each cage is the number of the corresponding cat.

When all cats are ready to be judged, the judge will begin his examination. Each cat will be taken out of the cage—by the judge or the steward—and situated on the little platform in the center of the table,

Gr. Ch. Sidarka Justa Jiffi, a successful English Blue Burmese owned by Mrs. Nunn and bred by Wendy Bookbinder. Jiffi's litter sister is Jenibeau Jangles, also a Grand Champion. Sire Gr. Ch. Sidarka Henry Hotfoot; Dam Ch. Sidarka Delta Dawn.

Pr. Sittang Berenice, an English neutered Blue Burmese owned by Jenny Cunningham and bred by the Rev. G. M. Briscoe and Mr. M. Kelly. Sire Sabra Blue Josephus; dam Ramree Sarana.

or the "ring." A thorough examination follows. After each examination the judge's hands as well as the table are disinfected. The final decision is reached by comparison and point evaluation against the breed standard; then the ribbons are awarded, and the cats retrieved by their proud (or disappointed) owners or agents. Four to six winner's ribbons, with minimum scores, are needed to become a champion in one day. An agreed number of final wins can earn the title of grand champion, provided the judging was done under different judges.

The cages behind the judge's table are disinfected, and a new group of anxious cat owners will be called. It goes without saying that the decision of the judge is always final!

Buskins Chantek, Brown Burmese, granddaughter of Ch. Sablesilk Mouse, owned by Mrs. Barbara Harrington and bred by Mrs. Nicki Horne.

Six
A Burmese or Malayan in Your Household

Whether it be adult or kitten, and whether the household previously included other Burmese, Malayan or other cats, the resulting rearrangements and alterations in the hierarchy (and to you) must be expected and noticed. Imagine a house where the owners have never had a Burmese or Malayan before. The preparations must be maximum, as they don't know what to expect. If the household is on ground floor level, they cannot for a period of several weeks open a door or a window more than 1½ inches, exit or enter a door without loud warning yells, or let a door shut without control. It is almost the same with an adult cat and there are stringent rules for when a cat is lost. Many clubs have written a leaflet to be handed to new owners. Decide beforehand which room you wish to be the cat's "anchor" room and prepare it by making it escape-proof, including the chimney; provide a good heated bed, a litter tray, water, toys, and cat grass.

Burmese and Malayan cats are great escapers and will get out of incredibly small and inaccessible openings. Having got out, they are capable of traveling in someone's car, only to emerge in a strange place, demanding a meal.

The cat may not use the room of your choice at all, and will only settle on, in or under your bed, or some precious antique (a habit easily formed). Make sure all breakable things are put away or fastened to something. These cats are incredibly clumsy when operating at top speed. They run up curtains and come down on your back when you are not expecting it. Certain items, such as telephone wires, must be especially protected from chewing. These cats do not hesitate to eat and drink from other people's and other animals' containers.

Burmese and Malayan cats live equally happily in a town apartment or on a country estate. The only requirement for the town cat is to have access to air, and many owners have contrived very imaginative runs built around windows or doors so that the cat is let out into a "cage within a garden." This seems to work admirably.

To compensate you for your cat's special demands, many are the times when your heart is turned by them, three or four together, licking each other, purring, then sleeping upside down, with feet in the air. They wake you by nuzzling or licking, most painfully but quite usually catching your nostril with a sharp claw. If you are ill, your bed is a very popular place for Burmese or Malayans and their peculiarly therapeutic, warm, and loving bodies.

Because the bone structure of the face of these breeds has not been changed, i.e., it has not been artificially flattened or lengthened, there is a charming but natural expression, with a retroussé nose and strong chin. The expression comes to you from under partly lowered eyelids, producing a slightly sullen look, known rather boastfully as a "Burmese or Malayan look." It is a reproachful look that asks for something that you cannot interpret, but it is probably attention. Frequently judges' reports mention the "Burmese or Malayan look," and we all recognize it, but find it difficult to define.

One member of a family of Burmese or Malayans will take over from another those duties that are undertaken by the senior of your household. It is curiously touching to notice that a granddaughter, on the loss of her grandmother, will take over cleaning, grooming, and training the younger feline members of the family.

It is sad to remember our cats as they look when very old, especially if old age is accompanied by illness. We should be happy to remember them young and in their prime. Old age comes to Burmese and Malayans with dignity and serenity, beautiful because if often reflects the pattern of their lives; they carry on the same little tricks of a lifetime, retrieving as they did when kittens, falling on their heads perhaps as an expression of affection.

Burmese and Malayan cats frequently live to the age of 16 or 17, and several recently have reached 19 or 20. They cannot go on being athletic champions, but they will continue their characteristic sociable mannerisms.

Burmese will not always do what you want them to. This Brown obviously finds the bird bath more exciting than her water bowl.

Opposite, left
A pleasant ride in the wheelbarrow.

Opposite, right
As soon as the telephone rings, this Brown Burmese stud, Ch. Indiaqueen Brown Bomber, knocks the receiver off as if to answer it. Owner Edward Young; breeder Pat Short.

Ch. Jingpaws Blue Monarch: although no longer with us, his progeny live on. Many of them are pictured in this book. Over the years he sired many famous and Champion cats, including the first Grand Premier English neutered Blue Burmese.

Seven

The Stud, the Queen, and Kittening

Perhaps one of the wisest of Burmese owners once said, "Your queen, your stud, and all the kittens you produce are members of your household and are your responsibility throughout their lives." Therefore, follow-up is necessary. Since no one should even think about owning a stud without long consideration and considerable breeding experience, we feel that one should start by keeping a queen and raising kittens.

To keep queens well, happy, and in excellent condition, they should not have more than three litters in two years, preferably fewer. Think also whether you can afford the money and the time to breed kittens. A working household finds it difficult to fit in extra feeding, correct weaning, visits to the veterinarian, and simply "being there." Breeding one's own queen to maturity is exciting: seeing her have her first litter and watching her suckle her first babies never ceases to be a wonderful experience, but it all takes a lot of time.

You will have had to select a stud long before the queen is mated. Obviously, he should be as good as possible an example

of Burmese or Malayan, but forgive us if we say you must also choose your stud owners carefully. If you are inexperienced, the stud owner should be patient, calm, quiet, and willing and able to give advice not only on the actual mating procedure but on forms, registration, transfer, and the appropriate types of vaccination. Equally, the stud should not be too young and inexperienced.

Keeping a Burmese or Malayan stud is an occupation that should not be entered into lightly, or the stud himself may become very unhappy and owners can be very unhappy too. Experience with kittening is essential. Even if you have chosen a well-reared kitten from a healthy line, and even if in his early career he has a successful list of queens waiting for his service, and has traveled to a number of shows and done well, there may come a period when his services go "out of fashion," and he will become lonely and miserable. He may be well looked after, fed and housed, but gradually isolation becomes the oustanding problem. Because of this, many Burmese and/or Malayan breeders have retired their hand-

some studs and, before it was too late, neutered them, and so turned them into delightful household companions. At the same time it would be wrong not to mention the close companionship a stud owner will have with the entire male over the years. One can spend many hours with him. Some owners set up sitting places in their stud houses, or have the stud where they can see him for a long part of the day.

Left
Gr. Ch. Rascals Butterscotch, a Red Burmese owned by Joyce Dell and bred by Jean Steward. Sire Ch. Kupro Red Lynx; dam Kupro Cream Conchita. Because of the black spots on the nose, this cat would be disqualified at an American show.

Right
Typha Mock Orange: when she was a kitten, many judges thought she had great promise, and indeed she holds two challenges certificates to date.

Chi Andromeda, a Malayan Champagne and the first Champion bred by Sandra Pightling, Sire Ch. Mibuya Le Marquis; dam Indina Virginia Fish.

54

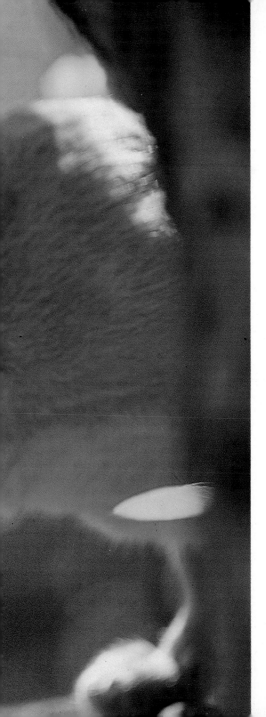

Care and Grooming

Writers on most breeds often describe in detail the way to groom and care for cats—this is particularly so with longhaired cats. With the Burmese and Malayan breeds it is difficult to do this in the same way.

The foremost requirement is a general appearance of well-being, and this is achieved by keeping the cat in a state of very good health. A Burmese or Malayan, due to its muscularity, is heavy for its size, and should "fill its coat," which will make it look glossy, the chief characteristic. Visit the veterinarian at once if you think something is wrong.

Although of course it is necessary to brush out dust and the hair of the old coat, it is unnecessary to brush and comb before shows; there are many breeders who say, "Leave it alone—do nothing. It will spoil the coat entirely if you keep on combing it." Some polish it with chamois leather, or a soft duster, but the majority of winners belong to owners who "do nothing." Of course, this does not mean that the cat should not have clean ears, dry eyes, clean nose, cut toenails etc., but these are all matters of good health and hygiene, not cosmetic treatment. Diets, both for cats and kittens, must be varied and sufficient. For detailed information on cat care, the reader is referred to the many excellent general books available.

Nine

The Future of the Breeds

The different cat clubs and societies all feel enthusiastic responsibility and deep affection toward the breeds. There are breeding programs drawn up and foundation stock carefully picked, not only for the desired colors, but also for health, strength, and stamina.

Quite a variety of colors have already been established, and as long as one looks after the maintaining of the basic character of the breeds, these exotic and gentle animals will remain unchanged.

Fortunately the increasing number of breeders have responsibly worked according to the standard. It is greatly to the credit of the really dedicated breeders that they guide their followers and set an example of integrity. From them there continue to emerge the group of well-informed cat fanciers, knowledgeable in genetics and cat husbandry.

In a book of this length we can mention only a few cats and prefixes, only some of those we have had an opportunity to see and know. There are many more that cannot be mentioned for lack of space, and it is on all these excellent studs and queens and respectable owners that the future of the breeds depends.

In Britain there are now brown, blue, chocolate, lilac, red and cream cats, and torties obtained from brown or chocolate and red, and from blue or lilac and cream.

In the United States, we have brown, red and tortie, and in the Malayan breed blue, champagne, and platinum. A few breeders have expressed interest in moving into other color fields, but there are as yet no recognized developments.

Most Burmese and Malayan breeders prefer to think that the future lies in the improvement of type, and concentration on the correction of faults shown in judges' reports, such as undershot chins, tail defects, disappearance of nose breaks, "Roman" noses, and the "bars" which still appear on the coat. What is quite clearly our ambition is to achieve, in any color, a "bar-free" coat, such as the beautiful clear coats already arrived at in the Cream Burmese in Britain.

Just one day old . . . what will the future hold?

57

Appendices

The Official Standards

Burmese

Point Score

Head (25)	
Roundness of head	7
Breadth between eyes	4
Full face with proper profile	8
Ear set and placement	6
Eyes (5)	
Placement and shape	5
Body (30)	
Torso	15
Muscle tone	5
Legs and feet	5
Tail	5
Coat (10)	
Short	4
Texture	4
Close-lying	2
Color (30)	
Body color	25
Eye color	5

General: The overall impression of the ideal Burmese would be a cat of medium size and rich solid color; with substantial bone structure, good muscular development and a surprising weight for its size. This, together with its expressive eyes and sweet face, presents a totally distinctive cat that is comparable to no other breed. Perfect physical condition, with excellent muscle tone. There should be no evidence of obesity, paunchiness, weakness, or apathy.

Head: Pleasingly rounded without flat planes, whether viewed from front or side. Face full, with considerable breadth between the eyes, tapering slightly to a short, well-developed muzzle. In profile there should be a visible nose break.

Ears: Medium in size and set well apart on a rounded skull; alert, tilting slightly forward, broad at base with slightly rounded tips.

Eyes: Set far apart and with rounded aperture.

Body: Medium in size, muscular in development, and presenting a compact appearance. Allowance to be made for larger size in males. An ample, rounded chest, with back level from shoulder to tail.

Legs: Well-proportioned to body.

Paws: Round. Toes: Five in front and four behind.

Tail: Straight; medium in length.

Coat: Fine, glossy, satinlike in texture; short and close-lying.

Color: The mature specimen should be rich, warm sable brown; shading almost imperceptibly to a slightly lighter hue on the underparts, but otherwise without shadings or markings of any kind. Nose leather: Brown. Paw pads: Brown. Eye color: Ranging from yellow to gold, the greater the depth and brilliance the better.

Penalize: Green eyes.

Disqualify: Kinked or abnormal tail. Locket or button. Incorrect number of toes. Blue eyes.

Malayan

Point Score

Head (25)
- Roundness of head — 7
- Breadth between eyes — 4
- Full face with proper profile — 8
- Ear set and placement — 6

Eyes (5)
- Placement and shape — 5

Body (30)
- Torso — 15
- Muscle tone — 5
- Legs and feet — 5
- Tail — 5

Coat (10)
- Short — 4
- Texture — 4
- Close-lying — 2

Color (30)
- Body color — 25
- Eye color — 5

General: The overall impression of the ideal Malayan would be a cat of medium size and rich solid color; with substantial bone structure; good muscular development and a surprising weight for its size. Perfect physical condition with excellent muscle tone. There should be no evidence of obesity, paunchiness, weakness, or apathy.

Head: Pleasingly rounded without flat planes, whether viewed from front or side. Face full, with considerable breadth between the eyes, tapering slightly to a short, well-developed muzzle. In profile there should be a visible nose break.

Ears: Medium in size and set well apart on a rounded skull; alert, tilting slightly forward, broad at base with slightly rounded tips.

Eyes: Set far apart and with rounded aperture.

Body: Medium in size, muscular in development, and presenting a compact appearance. Allowance to be made for larger size in males. An ample, rounded chest, with back level from shoulder to tail.

Legs: Well-proportioned to body.

Paws: Round. Toes: Five in front and four behind.

Tail: Straight; medium in length.

Coat: Fine, glossy, satinlike in texture, short and close-lying.

Penalize: Green eyes.

Disqualify: Kinked or abnormal tail. Locket or button. Incorrect number of toes. Blue eyes.

Malayan Colors

Champagne: The mature specimen should be a warm honey-beige, shading to a pale gold-tan underside. Slight darkening on ears and face permissible, but lesser shading preferred. A slight darkening in older specimens allowed, the emphasis being on evenness of color. Nose leather: Light warm brown. Paw pads: Warm pink-

The first female British Grand Champion Malayan Platinum Gr. Ch. Bambino Lilac Villow, with her daughter Bambino Villalicious: bred by Barbara Boizard.

ish tan. Eye color: Ranging from yellow to gold, the greater the depth and brilliance the better.

Blue: The mature specimen should be a medium blue with warm fawn undertones, shading almost imperceptibly to a slightly lighter hue on the underparts, but otherwise without shading or markings of any kind. Nose leather: Slate gray. Paw pads: Slate gray. Eye color: Ranging from yellow to gold, the greater the depth and brilliance the better.

Platinum: The mature specimen should be a pale, silvery gray with pale fawn undertones, shading almost imperceptibly to a slightly lighter hue on the underparts, but otherwise without shadings or markings of any kind. Nose leather: Lavender-pink. Paw pads: Lavender-pink. Eye color: Ranging from yellow to gold, the greater the depth and brilliance the better.

Ch. Vatan Cream Adonis, owned by Ann and Alan Fullwood and bred by Don Beech and Jim Chalmers. He has an interesting genetic makeup, being a cream homozygous for Platinum.

Genetics of the Burmese Cat

(Reprinted from the *Journal of Heredity*)

Joseph C. Thompson, Virginia C. Cobb, Clyde E. Keeler, and Madeleine Dmytryk
April 1943

The first "Burmese" cat was a female imported into the United States from Burma by the senior author in the year 1930. Its bodily conformation and behavior were typical for native Malay cat stocks, best represented in America by the Siamese variety. The Burmese was not recognized at once by the fanciers as a new breed, but suffered for some time the onus of being considered by most persons as an "off-colored Siamese." This explanation sounded very plausible to owners of Siamese who knew that usually the body color of the Siamese darkens with age and varies to a certain extent with the seasons of the year. To make matters worse, the first Burmese cat did not breed true, but threw both Burmese and Siamese kittens when mated to its nearest available Malay cat type, the Siamese.

Two of the present authors (C.E.K. and V.C.C.) at once recognized the first Burmese cat as belonging to a new "incipient true-breeding variety." On the basis of crosses made by the senior author and through a paper (by C.E.K. and V.C.C.) in 1934 one of us (V.C.C.) proposed[1] to the Cat Fanciers' Association that the Burmese be recognized as a new color variety for show purposes. Agitation was continued until its acceptance in 1936. Burmese are now eligible for registration in the Association Stud Book.

Further crosses by the senior author produced the foundation pedigree of the breed. Starting with the imported Burmese cat, Wong Mau, containing one gene for Burmese and one gene for Siamese, and by mating this to a Siamese, Tia, it has been possible to establish a Burmese variety that has bred true for three generations.

The official standards[2] for Burmese call for a Siamese conformation, a chocolate brown body color with seal points and topaz eyes. The kinky tail common to so many Malay cats has not been bred out of Burmese stock and is generally present.

It was recognized that Mendelian segregation of two coat colors was taking place in crosses of the imported Burmese to a Siamese male. The light-colored kittens always developed into typical sealpoint Siamese cats with china blue eyes and the dark kittens all became Burmese cats with topaz-colored eyes. There were no intermediate color gradations observed.

From crosses of this sort mde by the senior author, there resulted 11 Burmese males, 16 Burmese females, 11 Siamese males, and 10 Siamese females.

Mr. Mel Friedlander mated a Burmese female with a Siamese male. This cross produced four Siamese and four Burmese.

One of us (V.C.C.) crossed a Burmese female to a Siamese male. There resulted three Siamese and two Burmese. In all, such crosses have produced a total of 34 Burmese: 27 Siamese.

Because these four segregating classes were present in relatively equal numbers, it was suspected that they represented a monofactorial backcross involving one contrasted pair of autosomally borne gene alleles, or that some independent autosomal gene, manifest only in the presence of the Siamese pattern, was converting certain genotypically Siamese kittens into Burmese.

It soon became apparent that all genes involved must be autosomal because of the numerical equality of the sexes in both Siamese and Burmese categories. Thus, the possibility of the genetic complication of sex-linkage was readily dismissed.

It had been shown previously by two of the authors (C.E.K. and V.C.C.) that the gene producing "silver" or "smoke" in cats is an allele or alternative form of the same gene that produces the Siamese coat pattern. Both silver and Siamese coats are affected by temperature and age, and both types have points darker than the body color. This is more evident in the non-agouti or non-tabby form, namely smoke.

From the results of these experiments, coupled with the fact that the Burmese also has dark points and that the body coat darkens with age, it appeared that Burmese might well present a physiological intermediate between silver and Siamese. If a physiologically intermediate stage between these two coat colors, it appeared probable that it might be an allele. The breeding experiments were henceforth conducted to test this hypothesis.

If Burmese represents an intermediate allele between silver and Siamese, we can make the following predictions:

1. When Burmese is crossed to normal intensity all of the offspring will exhibit normal intensity of pigmentation.
2. When purebred Burmese is bred to Siamese, all the kittens should be Burmese.
3. All Siamese segregates from crosses involving Burmeses should breed true for Siamese.
4. When Burmese (whether purebred, or hybrid for Siamese) is mated to silver or smoke, the offspring should all be silver or smoke rather than tabby or black,

An example of a fine British Cream Burmese: Ch. Patriarca Passibury, owned by Ronnie Brooks and bred by Pat Brownsell.

tens so produced were of normal intensity. This confirms prediction No. 1.

It was learned that where there was opportunity for the Burmese gene to enter a cross from both parents, there might be in addition to Siamese kittens, two shades of Burmese kittens. The lighter of the two shades developed into the coat color of Wong Mau. The darker shade developed into a darker body color.

It is well known that in rabbits, rats, and mice an animal showing a member of the albino series of allelic coat colors will be lighter when hybrid for a lower allele than if purebred for the given first allele. Aware that we were probably dealing with alleles of the albino series in the cat, we suspected that these two types of Burmese represented animals purebred for the Burmese gene (darker) and hybrid for the Siamese gene (lighter), respectively. A cross of dark Burmese to Siamese yielded only Burmese kittens, in keeping with prediction No. 2.

Where two Burmese, each hybrid for Siamese, were mated, the 3:1 ratio was observed. The verification matings by one of us (M.D.) gave 20 Burmese : 5 Siamese. When these 20 Burmese were divided as to color phase, there were found 3 dark and 17 light. We actually expect twice as many light as dark for a Mendelian explanation.

Prediction No. 4 was the most difficult of all to test, because so many matings between Burmese and Smoke failed to produce offspring, to such an extent that it was suspected that some sort of physiological block prevented interfertility between these varieties. But the persistence of one of us (M.D.) eventually resulted in a fruitful mating. A Smoke-Persian female was mated to a Burmese (hybrid for Sia-

as is the case when animals bearing two Mendelian coat colors due to genes at independent loci are involved.

The stud, Pak Kwai Mau (Siamese segregate of the first Burmese, Wong Mau, by a Siamese sire, Tia Mau) has sired more than 500 kittens of Siamese queens. All of these kittens have been Siamese without a suggestion of Burmese. Nor have the authors ever heard of Siamese cats having Burmese ancestry throwing Burmese unless mated with Burmese. These facts are in line with prediction No. 3.

Burmese has been outcrossed to cats of normal coat color intensity. All the kit-

mese). Five kittens resulted, all smokes. This confirmed our final prediction No. 4.

Conclusion

Thus, we may conclude from the results of all our genetic tests that:

1. The Burmese is a distinct, new coat color variety of the domestic cat, having a sound genetic basis, in that dark Burmese will breed true.
2. The Burmese coat color is based upon the possession of a pair of Burmese genes (dark color phase) or of a single Burmese gene and its Siamese gene allele (light phase).
3. Burmese and Siamese genes are sharply contrasted in their effects, there being no intermediate grades of coat color observed and Mendelian ratios being found in both F^2 and backcross matings.
4. The Burmese gene represents a fourth identified allele in the albino series which, naming the genes in order of diminishing pigmentation produced, are as follows:

    1—Normal intensity (Tabby or Black)
    2—Silver (Smoke)
    3—Burmese
    4—Siamese

Postscript

A color variation darker than ordinary Siamese was discovered by Lelia Volk of Honolulu, to be segregating in her Siamese strain. This was examined by one of us (C.E.K.) and found to be intermediate in color between Burmese and Siamese, and hence we suspect the Hawaiian variation to represent a fifth allele in the albino series. It is so near Siamese in color, however, that it will probably not be perpetuated as a distinct variety, and hence the possibility will probably not be had of checking its genetic relationships. At least one intermediate allele between the one producing an intensity similar to that of Burmese and the one producing Himalayan is known in rabbits, and a similar gene[4] (extreme dilute of Detlefson) is known in mice. These facts seem to make our suspicion of the Honolulu variation representing a fifth albino series allele in cats seem even more plausible.

Literature cited

1. Report of New York Cat Show, *New York Times,* No. 23, 1934.
2. Standards for Burmese privately printed by Cat Fanciers' Association.
3. Keeler, Clyde E. and Virginia Cobb, *J. Hered.,* 25:181–4, 1933.
4. Detlefson, J. A., *Amer. Nat.,* 55:469–73.

Orphaned at birth, this brown kitten was raised by a bull terrier and her puppies.

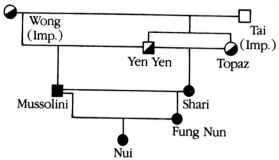

Foundation stock of the Burmese variety of cats.

Ch. Patriarca Preeming Patience, an English Chocolate Tortie owned by Mrs. A. Tate and bred by Pat Brownsell. Sire Patriarca Paddington Bear; dam Patriarca Perquita.

Squares represent males, and circles females. The solid black symbols indicate pure breeding Burmese. The half-shaded symbols indicate Burmese × Siamese hybrids which carry one gene for Burmese and are intermediate in color; the unshaded symbols indicate the pure Siamese.

The Tortoiseshell Factor in Burmese

(quoted by permission of the Burmese Cat Club)

When red or cream (cream is a dilution of the red) Burmese males are mated with any of the solid-colored females (i.e., brown, chocolate, blue, lilac), then a percentage of the resulting progeny will contain some Tortoiseshell females.

This is because the red gene, represented by the symbol O but referred to in genetics as 'yellow,' is sex-linked, meaning that it is carried by only one of the sex chromosomes, namely the X. A male has one X and one Y chromsome and a female two X chromosomes. Males can therefore only be O (yellow) or o (non-yellow) whereas females can be OO (yellow), Oo (Tortoiseshell) or oo (non-

yellow). The coat of the heterozygous female Oo shows the influence of the two genes by having both yellow and non-yellow areas of color, which is the characteristic of Tortoiseshell.

Now the O gene is affected by polygenes which deepen the color, so yellow cats may vary a great deal in the depth of color their fur shows. In the Tortoiseshells this will be seen as a variation in the red color. No two Tortoiseshells are alike either in depth of coat color or in the areas where the colors occur on the animal. Coloring may be patched, mingled or both, and one should never be surprised at the individual coloring of the Tortoiseshell; its pedigree will show which colors are genetically possible and they are not difficult to recognize.

Briefly, if a red male is used on a solid-colored female (non-red) the litter will not contain any red females. This is because the male can only transmit one sex-linked gene (O or o) in 50 per cent of gametes; the other 50 per cent receive a Y chromosome which does not possess an O gene. A red male mated to a brown Tortoiseshell however can produce a red female (OO).

Only four basic colors of Tortoiseshell Burmese are possible—brown, chocolate, blue and lilac—as the O gene has the same effect on all the solid colors, namely, to block the melanic pigment. But it is possible for a Tortoiseshell to display two shades of its basic colors. Thus a brown Tortoiseshell may seem to display four colors but in actuality these are two shades of red and two shades of brown.

A full color chart of possible matings which will produce the different colored Tortoiseshells, red and cream females, etc. can be had from the Burmese Cat Club.

Burmese Breed Clubs

Great Britain
The Burmese Cat Club
Secretary: Miss M. Silverman
Flat 6, 25 Shepherds Hill
London N. 6, England

Europe
No Burmese breed clubs.

United States
Burmese Limited
Irene Stolarz
168 Delavan Ave.
Newark, New Jersey 04104

National Burmese Cat Club
Mrs. Phyllis Sanftner
Normandy Heights Road
Morristown, New Jersey 07960

Northwest Burmese Fanciers
Linda Anderson
1985 SW 195
Aloha, Oregon 97005

Rocky Mountain Burmese Breeders
Mrs. Wayne E. Miller
814 Braemere Road
Boise, Idado 83702

Bay Area Burmese Breeders
Mrs. Dolores Campanile, Pres.
794 Hawthorne Drive
Walnut Creek, California 94596

Sabur Burmese Breed Club
Mary Holloway
2136 Byron Rd.
Sacramento, California 95825

Burmese Breeders
Mary Jane Eaton
Route 1
Stillwater, Oklahoma 74074

Cardinal State Burmese Fanciers
Mrs. Joyce Casto
Route 2, 1870 E. Powell Rd.
Westerville, Ohio 43081

Index

Page numbers in bold type refer to illustrations

BURMESE AND MALAYAN CATS is one of a series of new books written by connoisseurs for the genuine cat lover.

MOIRA K. SWIFT, formerly a Committee Member of the Burmese Cat Club, England, is one of the best respected judges of the breeds.

DR. MATTHEW VRIENDS is a well-known biologist with many books on pets to his credit.

The book describes the history and development of Burmese and Malayan cats in all their colors, from the original Brown, to the Malayan Blue, Champagne, Platinum, Red, and Tortie. There are sections on showing, breeding, keeping the breeds in the household, and care and grooming.

A particular feature of the book is the detailed information on Burmese and Malayan genetics, now and during the development of the breeds.

Over 40 color photos, most of them of outstanding cats, show the reader what to aim for in a Burmese or Malayan breeding program.

Cover illustrations: front, Benjamin Brown (Brown Burmese) and Love-in-the-Mist (Malayan Blue), both owned by Moira K. Swift; back, Typha Mock Orange (Malayan Platinum)
Photos: Paddy Cutts/Animal Unlimited

42 illustrations, including 41 in color

A BARRON'S BOOK

Also published by Barron's:
Longhair Cats by Grace Pond
Siamese Cats by Mary Dunnill